Poetry U.S.A.

KEVIN BOWEN

EIGHT TRUE MAPS OF THE WEST

The Dedalus Press

EIGHT TRUE MAPS
OF THE WEST

poems by

Kevin Bowen

To my only inspiration
+ keeper of my heart
I Love you So much. Thank
you for making this
book so beautiful
+ my life. Your soul mate
+ husband

Kev
5/19/03

DEDALUS

Dedalus Dublin 2003

The Dedalus Press
24 The Heath ～ Cypress Downs ～ Dublin 6W
Ireland

ISBN 1 904556 04 3

Cover Painting: "Croghaun Mountain"
by Leslie Bowen

for Winnie Fenton

The Dedalus Press gratefully acknowledges permission to reprint poems from Kevin Bowen's earlier books: *Playing Basketball with the Viet Cong* and *Forms of Prayer at the Hotel Edison*, both published by Sandy Taylor and Judy Doyle of Curbstone Press. New poems have appeaared in *Cimarron Review, Intervention, Field, Massachusetts Review,* and *Witness.*

The author wishes to acknowledge the support of the Massachusetts Cultural Council and the National Endowment for the Arts.

Dedalus Press books are represented and distributed in the UK by **Central Books**, 99 Wallis Road, London E9 5LN and in the U.S.A. and Canada by **Dufour Editions Inc.**, PO Box 7, Chester Springs, Pennsylvania 19425

The Dedalus Press receives financial assistance from
An Chomhairle Ealaíon, The Arts Council, Ireland

Printed in Dublin by Johnswood Press

CONTENTS

New Poems : Eight True Maps of the West

from

PLAYING BASKETBALL WITH THE VIET CONG

FIRST CASUALTY

They carried him slowly
down the hill.
One hand hung,
grey and freckled.
No one spoke but
stared straight up.
His body, heavy,
rolled back and forth
on the litter.
At LZ Sharon cooks spooned
the last hot food.
One by one the squad
walked back up hill.
"Don't mean nothing,"
someone said.
But all that winter
and into spring
I swear he followed us,
his soul, a surplice
trailing the jungle floor.

CITIES OF DUST

The click of footsteps down the hall,
high spiked heels on marble.
The shower running in the room next door.
Four a.m. The first night you never sleep,
air thick with gas and dust, flames
from street stalls, satay burning and sex
on stage and in back-street rooms.
The traffic could bury you here, mad orchestra of horns,
trucks, cars, motorcycles, the old elephant transport
reduced to bright colours of tuk tuks.
The unexpected always coming head on.
A barker on the street unfolds his wallet,
three naked girls leer from a white tub.
Their poses, the distraught angles, mimic postures
of dancers carved on sandstone temples an hour's drive away.
Turn and he's gone. Only traffic, the click of heels
(you know the sound), a life disappearing in dust and haze.

War Story for Paul

Let me tell it for you.
This time we'll try to get it right.
You're in the mountains,
come to a meadow.
You hesitate, you've seen it all
before, but decide to take the risk.
You take the first step out into the clearing,
and there they are,
twenty, maybe more,
their leader, the largest, in front.
He raises his fist.
He first, then all of them
the whole troop of rock apes,
beat the ground with two-foot clubs,
their eyes burn straight through you.
A mistake. You try to run,
but your legs won't budge.
Then suddenly they break free
and you're running down a trail,
but too soon it becomes the trail
of another story and a wooded ridge
above a river where you raise the wounded
into the liftship again. Each body
oozes white pus
you can't get off,
no matter how you try.
You run down the hill to the river,
roll in the sand hoping to beat
the flies and the smell and scum away,

but can't until you've torn every bit
of clothing off and run
naked in the stream toward me.

RAPPELLING
Camp Evans, 1968

We dive happily.
No good-byes,
one last look at the sergeant
and then over the edge
of the tower,
down ropes burning fast
through hooks.
The secret, not to panic,
to give in to desire
to clutch the line connects
the world above
to the one below
and so smash head first
against the wooden piles.
After the first fear,
there is calm
floating down,
hit the ground
run backwards tiptoe,
untangle the line for the next boy
and the next,
now descending all
four sides of the tower,
whirling like stars
out into the jungle.

FERRY CROSSING NORTH OF HAI PHONG

"a traveller's heart is rinsed in fresh waters" - Li Po

Up and down the coast
sampans sit becalmed,
red notes on a green-bannered sea.
Sounds of banging tin drums
drift down river,
mix with calls of women
hanging wash from fishing boats.
At the crossing, two trucks
overloaded with coal from the northern ranges
have driven the ferry aground
twenty yards from shore.
Children from fields,
feet caked with paddy mud,
cut back and forth across dikes.
Passengers throng the road
that runs out to greet them
lined with coconuts, oranges,
sweet bananas, loaves of bread.

At the water's edge an old man
stacks green bottles in rows
until they rise in entreaty.
Children stretch under trucks,
gather coal dust
to mix with dung
women carve in wheels by the road.
Nothing is wasted.

By the checkpoint, a crone
sings an old folk song,
but keeps losing the words.
She has no destination but crossing
back and forth,
each time, she says, to die.
Thirty yards away, the captain
tries to guide the ferry to shore.
He runs from bow to bridge,
checking depth,
the engine's temper. He backs off
the bank, assembles
the passengers in the stern.
The boat floats free.
Chains grind, tug
tightens to barge, the deck
a faded wash of blue
uniforms, eyes
pleading for rescue
as he hits the throttle
and the engine stalls.
The ferry drifts into swells,
currents circling out to sea.
From shore, passengers
watch a second tug
cut loose its cargo,
nose into the river
downstream. Two boats
maneuver against mountains,
river and sky.

This time the weight of the second tug

sends the barge to land.
Bikes and trucks and bodies
merge, push off, then part,
each to their destinations.
River and road break free.

INCOMING

Don't let them kid you —
The mind's no fool like the movies,
doesn't wait for flash or screech,
but moves of its own accord,
even hears the slight
bump the mortars make
as they kiss the tubes good-bye.
Then the furious rain,
a fist driving home a message:
"Boy, you don't belong here."
On good nights they walk them in,
you wait for them to fall,
stomach pinned so tight to ground
you might feel a woman's foot
pace a kitchen floor in Brownsville;
the hushed fall of a man lost
in a corn field in Michigan;
a young girl's finger trace
a lover's name on a beach along Cape Cod.

But then the air is sucked
straight up off the jungle

floor and the entire weight
of Jupiter and her moons
presses down on the back of a knee.
In a moment, it's over.
But it takes a lifetime to recover,
let out the last breath
you took as you dove.
This is why you'll see them sometimes,
in malls, men and women off in corners:
the ways they stare through the windows in silence.

TEMPLE AT QUAN LOI, 1969

Outside the gate
the old woman
walks up the hill
from the temple.
Her pace
deliberate as a procession.
From the corner of an eye
she stares.
She must wish our deaths.
Beneath the white silk band
breasts ache for a husband.
She passes in mourning,
counting each step.
Her prayers rain down like rockets.

Branded Kraits

Blackburn saw him first,
called us over
just as he poked his head up,
four of us
hovering over the hole
at the bottom of the slumped pile
of sandbags
at the old French base camp.
He lingered a second,
then quick as it took
to take our measrue,
squrimed back down,
flipping his tail at us
as if in some obscene gesture.
But already the gasoline
was on its way. Morales
held the five-gallon can
carefully over the hole
as we watched to see
if the snake would crawl out again
as gas sifted into dirt
and the thin slit in the earth
that was his home
disappeared and reappeared
in slow migrations of sand
that seemed the pulse
of somebody's heart
we couldn't remember
until Morales dropped a match

and the blaze slunk down
the hole after.
He came out slowly.
One good shot
straight through the head
put him away.
We laid him out,
all four feet of him and fangs.
Enough time to smoke a cigarette
was what he'd give you.
The same that we gave him.
Then, babies, someone said.
We smoked and joked
our way to the green line.
Cambodia, the rains, June's weeping light.

MISSING

How you put those dots together and got Beethoven
was a mystery. Third grade nuns didn't teach you that.
Or how it was you were home when the TV host called
so you could yell the answer to your grandmother,
who looked blankly at the screen, not half-believing
the man in there could be the same one on the phone.
Back in Scotland, in the village where she came from,
things didn't happen like that.

You won three Edsels and a trip to Disneyland.
Then in California, on another quiz, you won prizes
for your sister, who was not that sick.
Your parents bought a summer house that year.
We charged your boat across the lake.
Nights, we snuck in back of the Casino,
watched your cousin dance in tight black slacks.
Our world was movies and rollerskates, shooting
bb's at dogs, and taking lessons in sex from the locals.
Mornings, behind the lake we hunted frogs for bait,
stuck our hooks down long green spines
to lure the pickerel. The force of the strike
still wakes me late at night.
What came between us I don't remember,
only getting on the bus, and the call,
my brother sick.

I followed your story after that.
Military school, marriage to an heiress.
Someone said you'd tried to kill yourself,

I doubted it, at least your luck had saved you
until that pilot caught you in his sights
over Ha Long Bay. What did you think
as you fell, the cars, the boats,
the girls, the picture of a boy
on the mantle in kilts?
Whose face did you see
mapped across the sky?
I was there that day, felt the tug,
looked down and saw my own face
looking up to me from the paddy,
searching the sky where already you'd disappeared.

THIEN QUANG LAKE

Beneath the window, the street sweeper
makes his slow morning pass around the lake.
Lights of the V.I.P. Club
burn amber in trees by the guest house
where the power has just returned,
the fan lifting the thick night air.

On a long journey I have woken
many times in the night
dreaming of the ones I love.

Deep in the dark of the room,
I turned to find them in postures
I know best. One kissed me deep
on the throat. One clapped
from a bed. One opened a door to my room.

What I didn't know was how far
we take the ones we love
into our bodies, how deep
we carry them until they call out
on nights like this, on a lake
whose name is the Buddha's Light.

THE ARTS OF LOVE AND HYDROLOGY
AS PRACTICED IN HA NOI

for Thuy

During the monsoon
in the North she digs
a hole outside
the stucco complex
where she shares
a nine-square-meter flat
with her father, mother,
and younger brother.
In the mornings at five,
she rises from her
hammock and begins
her chores before leaving
for the ministry.
Last, she dips the jars
of smoky glass down
into a fetid pool,
sets them by the hearth
then takes the route
she always has,
past the old school and canal.

It seems so distant now
that day she dove and dove
for him. She'd been
among the first pulled
back from the canal,
the bombs still falling.

They couldn't understand her
as she gestured
back to the water.
Then she left them, dove back in,
found him, drew him
up the bank where she pumped
the brackish waters
from her brother's chest.
Some of the children trampled,
she later learned, rushing from road
and school into the flooded ditch.

Still, evenings she returns
the same way; arriving home
again she checks to see
if the clay has settled
in the jars so she can cook.
Some nights the hues of crimson
in the rice will trouble
her as she lies in her
hammock dreaming late
of a lover laying
fresh-water pipe across
the broad green
fields of the delta.

BANKING LESSON, 1970

Your hero's welcome was cleaning
floors at the local bank
for minimum wage.
A little joke to start the day,
leaning on a pole, a train
rumbling through a tunnel,
a blue janitor's uniform from Sears
replacing olive green.
You were reading Stendhal,
stuck in your back pocket like a confession.
Each day, seven a.m., you began your tour
sweeping tape across the computer room,
everyone watching, you could tell.
Knock first before checking
the washrooms for paper stock,
empty trash pails for executives.
If they knew the murder in your head . . .
Lunch was a cafeteria filled
with girls in six-inch heels
and men in blue suits.
You ached as you passed through the line.
Back by the loading docks
you smoked your wrath up,
watched armoured trucks bring
the day's deposits from the branches.
How far could you get, you wondered,
Wednesdays mopping the main vault,
stacks of bills rising in piles on the walls.
How far?

PLAYING BASKETBALL WITH THE VIET CONG
for Nguyen Quang Sang

You never thought it would come to this,
that afternoon in the war
when you leaned so hard into the controls
you almost became part of the landscape:
just you, the old man, old woman
and their buffalo.
You never thought then
that this grey-haired man in sandals
smoking Gauloises on your back porch,
drinking your beer, his rough cough
punctuating tales of how he fooled
the French in '54,
would arrive at your back door
to call you out to shoot some baskets, friend.
If at first he seems awkward,
before long he's got it down.
His left leg lifts from the ground,
his arms arch back then forward
from the waist to release the ball
arcing to the hoop, one, two. . .
ten straight times. You stare at him
in his tee shirt, sandals, and shorts.
Yes, he smiles. It's a gift,
good for bringing gunships down
as he did in the Delta
and in other places where, he whispers,
there may be other scores to settle.

A CONICAL HAT
for Le Cao Dai and Vu Giang Huong

A moment of awkwardness
as he bends to lift the gift
to the table, not as if
he could hide it, the broad
conical shape of the "non la"
stared up at us all through dinner,
the girl who served us
stepping around it
as if to draw attention all the more.

Across the table all night
I watch the stories
come alive in his eyes;
I can almost see the bulb burning;
a man pedals a bicycle underground,
in the shadows of the bunker
he makes power for lights and suction
in the operating room.
Lungs burn, he inhales
fine red bits of earth.
They are digging to expand the tunnels,
make more room for the wounded.

A figure in white
draws a suture through
last bits of skin,
prays his sight holds.

One day he walks
straight off the earth,
right into the brown, wrinkled
hide of an elephant,
carves meat for a starving platoon,
takes machete and scalpel,
makes cut after cut
until he's covered
in blood and muscle,
fighting for air.

1970. A break in the fighting.
A game of volleyball, interrupted.
A gunship sprays the pitch.
Two nurses killed, he drags
their bodies down, heavy
and smoking, into the tunnels.

Ten years, his wife
slept in mountain caves,
after bombs, repaired roads,
made posters, paintings
to record each detail.

"Ham Rong Bridge, 1970," he shows me.
A woodcut on rice paper.
Two women in conical hats
load rocks along a road.
In the background trucks
grow wings of camouflage,
rattle across the bridge
heading south.

His eyes burn as he looks
through the woodcut.
I thank him. I will need this hat,
the cool circle of its shade.

ON MAI HAC DE

Late at night,
the good whiskey slips sure under the tongue.
The Ha Noi women, they can kill you with a look.
We watch them drive by on their bicycles,
their backs so stiff.
They have to know we're staring.
We are men gone soft with whiskey and dogmeat,
talking of ordinary things.
How we miss our wives, the warmth of a rice bowl,
the rain slipping slowly down the street.

SONG IN THE GREEN LIGHT
for Ha Khanh Linh

A young girl sings in the green light,
songs of leaves on the river, evening rain.
She strains to keep time with the boy
who fights the feedback of his bass.
Her voice, so clear, holds the strength
of her song high out over the audience,
men, women, and children who've come to the hall
drawn by the songs piped over loudspeakers.
In rumpled shirt and tie, her teacher
stands nervously to the side as the boy
at his feet changes the spotlight
from green to red, exposes a cracked
plaster wall, paintings by children where
boats drift on black rivers,
villages hang suspended under October moons.
The sadness of autumn gathers here.
I remember your words:
"Hope is an unharvested field."

RIVER MUSIC

One by one the lanterns
swim off down river.
A green one first, then red
and yellow. Each one calls
back a friend. Like dancers
they turn in circles.
One for my wife, one for my son,
one for our new child in spring.
Back and forth they swing
in twos and threes, seeking
evern newer combinations.
We drink rice liquor, toast
ten reasons men fall
in love on a river.
The old men smile into their instruments.
A woman sings, such beauty
even the moon might die
on her shoulder.

from

FORMS OF PRAYER AT THE HOTEL EDISON

DRIVING HOME

Out all night drinking
but not drunk.
Sent home by friends,
the round yellow pill
still on my tongue.

The car swings out
into the deep blue light,
wet splatter
of tire and asphalt.

Across the hills,
a thousand miles to Georgia.
McQuiston that June,
Caspar in fall,
just back from the jungle,
a blue truck flying
into brown mesas.

Is this what it's like?

I was running the hills
of Ohio when
my brother went off the road.
I watched a herd of deer
rush out from the woods
run right up to me
then veer off again
into the forest.

For a moment I thought
I was running with them,
hoofs just missing my feet,
their sweet moss blackened breath.

So close, I could have given
them names.

SAILING TO THAI BINH

Who would have thought so much cold
this far south? Early morning, we drive
Route Five, the great wide mouth
of the Red River opening out before us.
Dark brown fields hang in the mist,
stretch to the vanishing point.
The farmers who work them have bent
their thin bodies already for hours to earth.
They wear red bandannas around their necks,
bundle for warmth in the rhythm
of flood and mud and rain,
planting the last winter rice.
Three centuries since men and women
cut out a road from here to drag
a new bell for Keo Pagoda.
They laboured so hard to set it
gently in the wooden tower
high above the lily pond,

last carved their names in bronze, then turned,
foot by foot to cover the road over again.
Thirty nine stones in the temple well,
each one knocked hollow hammering
grain to feed the workers.
From here the French hung bodies
as warnings by the side of the road,
lifted whole villages to the mountains.
From here Bui Vien picked up his small bundle,
walked the long road south,
sailed a year around the world,
to step into Tyler's office,
beg him to send the French away.
From here a boy crossed from a buffalo's back,
looked down at his fields from the moon.

LETTER FROM THE NORTH
for B.W. and P.T.D.

In wet fields the farmers' cramped
hands clutch fast to their hoes.
We tumble through stone-coloured flesh.
All night the plane floating up over the oceans,
unknown lives passing through us.
So many. Barely enough time to say the names.
Gone, as if taken by a huge grey
hand entering a station, or those boats
with makeshift heads
nosing the stairs by the river.
This morning I turned the corner at Bui Thi Xuan
and walked into a funeral. The great black
bus without doors sailed past me,
the white banded mourners, red flags
leading drummers to the lake.
What is it we have seen
that we must travel so far to pray?

On May Hac De last night
I sat with the old men
in the slow dripping rain
and watched the cards fall in the dark.
Someone called my name, from the darkness,
I turned too late.
The gate creaked closed, a shadow
moving in the smoke of a kerosene lamp.
Outside the Apocalypse Bar, tourist buses
lined up on their way to the snake restaurant.

A young girl and her brother huddled in jackets
over a charcoal fire. They offered their warmth for sale.
A wooden bench, brandy, Laotian tobacco, strong tea.
Mutes, I sat and watched them sign in the darkness,
faces screwed up into those unsayable syllables,
bodies twisting, arms turned up, bent like ancient
wrestlers or those gods carved on old temple ceilings,
or the hump-backed man, two birds on his shoulders
by the yellow wall at Tran Quoc Pagoda.
On Hang Vai St., the wedding procession
stopped to light fireworks.
In the narrow street of restaurants, rockets
flew up in the air, drawing whole families out
to see the hissing snakes' heads of the flares,
the green and yellow sparks falling on tin rooftops.
Ba Chua Lieu, she came in a red dress first.
At her shrine I watched a soldier
burn money in a pit for his lost companions.
Time, he said. That's all.
In the story everyone already knew
the young girl was Lan Co, the old King's daughter.
The third time she came
she was dressed in white at Ho Tay.
This is why my friend told me in the small boat
that took us there, boat rocking in the misty waters,
the early morning fog, the great fields of birds spread
like beggars fingers calling from the lake.
Oh my friends, if they keep coming
I think their shadows will make a bridge
even our poor souls could cross.

Pho Hai Ba Trung

At the pagoda of the sisters
two women in brown suits
count out the day's receipts.

From bright red curtains
a white horse peers out behind them,
his paint so slowly peeling.

The old men on the steps
flap their arms as if
to fend off the bad weather,

their pockets stuffed with camellias.
On the street by the lake,
rows of women slake mud

washed up from storms,
mist rising off their backs.
So beautiful, you can almost see

the old gods descending,
curling up into the exact
ends of their fingertips.

SUNDAY AT THE MINAUN

Bobby Sands picture above the bar,
the green white scarf draped over his too young face.

In Kinshasa last night, two hundred killed.
In the morning paper a photo of a rebel in an alley

shooting one of Mobuto's sad-faced soldiers.
How many know why they fight?

In the North whispers of peace talks,
of how the parties will meet at a secret location

but will not have to speak.
Minaun looking down. The goat, in Irish.

I too once prayed for a miracle, but all I got
was a red chair moving across the room,

a newspaper opening its pages
to all the wrong answers.

Fregan. Answer.
Tomorrow the Chinese take back Hong Kong.

But still the Tutsis have nowhere to go. Their hungry,
dying faces linger in the low light of the bar.

Sunday rains driving the families in:
parents and children seeking shelter after mass.

So little light. Yesterday, the sheep looked at me
as if there was something I should know.

The lambs flitting back and forth across the road.
So far away, everything happening

as if through the lens of a slow motion camera.
As if all love had gone out of the world.

INCHEMEKINNA

I never asked how it was that when the Hunger came
they all went to the island;
or how they could survive on that small slip
of broken rock and green,
only a quarter mile across, a half mile long.
Never a good place to land a boat;
no sure footing.
Southwest, looking to the Arans, the single high point,
no more than twenty feet above the tide.
A few low, sloping trees.
But all around the island's waist
the kelps' rocky harvest, the razor necks,
shells rising up like white, speckled hands
to draw the gulls and birds
whose leavings made the beds deep and safe,
sent the flowers crawling up in terraces
the whole eastern side of the island.

The houses abandoned now,
chimneys crushed,
five, counting the one I stand in.
The shadow of its fires still black
against the back room wall,
the room where Bríd, the last to die here, was waked,
long lines of men and women
sailing in from Gorumna, Lettermore, and Spiddal,
wet scarves dripping up the path all afternoon.

BECAUSE WE WERE NOT HOME
for Winnie and Peggy

When you came by we were out
following the shepherd as he
climbed the rock cliffs at Keel.
He was leading his sheep up
the path by the falls, walking
them one by one as if he were
leading them into some picture
or painting. His small white dog
ripped and cut at their heels,
pushed them deep up
in line along the brown slope.
They moved together as if
under one of those glass spheres
you place on the mantle.
We climbed through wet moss

and rock, looking to find the high
ground, cut back and forth
across the nubs and rivulets,
trying to find the cutbacks to the old paths.
Half-way up, when we turned
we saw the sunlight like a beacon
slipping down from the clouds
onto the cold turquoise sea,
the sheep fields washed in its yellow light,
the soft greens and whites, the red door
of Michael Carr's house, his blue-eyed dogs
run wild in the yard.
What we thought a cemetery
was only another sheep field
at the top of a hill. We walked
the long path back, the children
threw rocks along the beach,
too late we found your note under the door.
Sorry we missed you, it said —
driving all the way from Carraroe
to let us know the phones
were out, you were leaving on Sunday,
hoped we would be enjoying our stay.

A GRANITE STAIRWAY: St Joseph's School for Boys

So many lives pressed into stone.
No vacant moments but always the praying,
praying for the right words to come.
For forgiveness. Always, the Nine am
rush of cassocks along the rails,
boys off to mass and funerals.
Afternoons, air raid drills,
cold dark walls against legs,
dreaming the flash of the bomb,
the heavy tomb like quiet,
a litany of names called into darkness:
Jackman, Kussy, Macaroni,
Bedugnis, Fitzgibbon, Pienisuski,
Salvator Bordinaro.
Boys whose fathers
worked at the post office,
bakery, track, the shoe store.
Boys down on their knees
praying for the war not to come,
for Russia's conversion.
Boys stepping off into a grey mist
to lead the procession each spring,
listening one more time
to the story of a girl in France,
and three children in Portugal,
who'd seen the Virgin;
and of one who carried a message to the Pope
who had yet to reveal its secret.

FATHER SEGADELI SAYS
SEVEN O'CLOCK MASS AT ST. JOSEPH'S

We kneel in the cold wooden pews
of the basement church of St. Joseph's.
Father Segadeli is lost again.
Somewhere between Lombardy and Korea
he has left us.
Maybe it was a noise from in the back
of the church that set him off,
but now he is off, lost in some world half-way
between the Mass of the Communicants
and the Mass of the Faithful.
His six-foot-nine-inch frame,
hunched over the tabernacle,
rises in a low moan as
he moves back from the altar.
He knows he must say the words as they were given.
Et introibo ad altare dei.
He begins the mass again.
I will go unto the altar of god.
No one leaves.

FRANCIS

The children found you. Christmas morning.
The far corner of the park.
Two days you lay there,
the voice on the radio said,
behind the abandoned Buick,
your body set on fire half a dozen times
before it finally caught.
A man wearing a dress.

Too soon the old words rolling off the tongue.
Faggot. Homo. Queen.
Sunday mornings
we watched you stroll to the altar,
bleached hair tossed back, like Monroe's in *The Misfits*.
Your face made-up in mascara, false lashes,
you held your chin forward like a gift.
We waited wondering would you fall,
the host sear off your tongue.

Whatever burned inside you, Francis,
they felt they needed a fire to kill.
In the snow your struggle left a black star.

FORMS OF PRAYER AT THE HOTEL EDISON

Last days before the war,
midnight, the end of his shift,
I watch him step out from the darkness
under the hotel canopy
into the streetlight's glare.
Night clerk in a dying city.

I know his feet must ache, standing all night,
watching the prostitutes, junkies, cops.
Some nights I think I see tears in his eyes,
maybe from the cold,
or a gas release from the chemical plant.

When he takes his place in the front seat of the car,
I crawl over into the back to sleep on the drive home,
listen to a man on the radio say he doesn't believe
in that place where already too many are dying.
In the windshield's reflection,
I see my father's beautiful hands, praying.

BUYING MY BROTHER A SUIT

In the old days they'd open the stores
on Sundays and holidays
if you called.
But today is Friday,
and I have come to buy
a suit for my brother
who never owned a suit,
my brother, who drove a cab nights
and in the day
cared for the sick and the crazy.
He would laugh if he saw me here.
But this is the way we live:
we take care of our own.
So I have come to buy my brother a suit,
to slip his long arms in one last time,
blue to match his eyes.
Later tonight, after
the mourners arrive,
and the room is full,
all of us remembering
what we loved best,
I will walk up to him
to check the line of his tie,
my sisters beside me,
nodding their approval.

BROTHERS

That time of year again
I feel you slowly moving in my body,
blood in blood.

I look in the mirror at my nakedness,
it is your girth I see,
your eyes
looking back at me,
looking into my face,
face which my friends
tell me, each day becomes
more and more
like yours.

So beautiful,
the way we grow into
each other's bodies,
how we never really part,
but spread out into
each other's lives.

What one day I had forgotten,
one night, looking out over the river
I hear you whisper
back to me.

This year, more and more,
I have come to know
how much the dead

inhabit me,
how at night and even
in the daytime
they come to me,
bringing me poems,
nudging me,
this thing, this thing you have
forgotten.

FOR MYLES WHO COMMUNES WITH PLANES

In the backyard I hold him up.
Nine months old, already his hand slaps out

the tempo of a vicious dribble.
Basketball, his great passion,

until a plane nears overhead.
He stirs before we even hear it,

flinches as if he knows it's there
before it flies in view.

He makes a rite of its passing.
First he turns, searches the sky,

seeks the strand of light in the distance,
then waves, pours a stream of wondrous

babble. I follow his lead, search,
point and smile. But what it is he's thinking

still eludes me. Is it joy he finds
in an image? A kind and gentle

god he sees up there? Or are they
faces of souls he recognizes,

disguised, bearing familiar features
from other lives?

Does he think it some small bird
he begs to descend, to land and

rest on the outstretched finger
of the hand he points?

Or is it finally some memory
from the womb he celebrates?

A last recollection, hum and image,
the moment of his leaving, brightness,

and that first great mystery of flight?

NEW POEMS

EIGHT TRUE MAPS OF THE WEST

Once More Again

Once more again the body counts on the news,
the hungry armies moving across the desert.

I hear a plane drone overhead and think of fuel
seeping down air shafts,
the loneliness of death anywhere.

Today the Head of Homeland Security
says the country is on Yellow Alert & the government
has retreated to shelters in the mountains.
The generals take orders to the beat of an old pacemaker.

What can or cannot be said anymore is not easy to decipher.

Part of you has already left this place.
Part of you struggles to hold on.

BROTHER TURTLE

I did it because he asked,
and I wanted to be a good guest.

So I drank the blood and ate the flesh,
then waited, but nothing happened.

The fish weren't biting
& the only one who spoke
was the small, wide-faced man
who straggled up the road
as we were drifting off to sleep.
He showed us pictures
of his two brothers
killed in the war
& told us how the Party
wanted to take back his land,
his small suburban fish pond
for some official's small profit.

But we were drunk on turtle blood vodka
& could not believe those were real tears
in his eyes
or in the eyes of the portraits
of his two brothers.

Brother Turtle, why did I not recognize you?

Now your tears run through me
& I know I will drown before I ever reach land.

MEDITATION AT THE END OF THE YEAR

New Year's Eve, a full moon low over the bay.
Along the canals, Christmas lights
hang like prayer beads on boats and homes.
Already the walkers are out, their soft words
drifting over the Pacific.
A lone helicopter curls back
and forth across the island,
drops lower and lower each time.

Somewhere in the darkness, the homeless
are just starting to sleep their hunger off,
a famous boxer is being chased by the police.

In Little Saigon, the presses sigh off
twenty years of exile.
As a great golden fish weaves up the Grand Canal
where John Wayne's yacht waits resurrection on the Lido.

In Santa Ana the police have broken into a party.
Don't move they say, but José, who knows no English
moves, and someone has to shoot him.
A search reveals no drugs or weapons.
On the highway, the strange shadow pictures
of families, their arms linked together,
crossing the road like deer.

Dioxin

Somewhere in the sky their healthy bodies float above us.
Somewhere they swim in an air better than any
we will ever know. The chemical scent gone, the burning.

Children sent back to live this time in their true bodies,
their pure, unsullied bodies, nothing in their cells
but the clear waters they see falling at the edge of the sky.

How many of them? How many each day slipping
out from flesh: children born into those twisted forms,
children with fins where arms might be, toes and legs

sprouting like flowers from their chests?
In a film, I watched two boys with giant heads,
heavy ovoid eyes, snouts for noses, sit gently

before a thatched house in a village. Eighteen and twenty
years old, still poised like children, they edged in close
beside their father who spoke with absolute calm about

the ways he cared for them. Moments later, a young woman
with clear, dark eyes leaned forward, tried to smile
but couldn't. All through the interview she struggled

patiently to get her two daughters, born without eyes,
to sit up straight on the mat beside her. — What many
forms love takes. — A friend told me once

the story of the birth of his son: how he climbed
the wall of the hospital so he could look in on his wife & child.
He was so filled with joy he said, to see them healthy,

he was half- way home before he realized he hadn't
checked to see if the baby was a boy or girl.
He asked if I had ever seen the fetuses

kept in jars in the hospital in the south,
those babies with the wizened faces
staring out through the yellow glaze of formaldehyde.

The image of their gorgon heads, their humped
and fish-like torsos woke him
up at night, he said.

Somewhere they too float in the sky above us.
Somewhere what doesn't die
lives on in silent rage.

OCEAN'S EDGE, BUNNACURRY

The music of the wind off the bog.
A sound so familiar, like the call of
an animal you once knew but had to leave
for a reason you no longer remember,
or the sound of a friend struggling,
lost deep in the jungle, calling out in the night.
Strange how everything arrives
to find its place in the end.

Even the cold bleeding body of the old red Ford,
its rotting chasis parked at the shoreline,
its seats still packed tight with passengers;
red, green, yellow plastic bags of turf,
those almost human shapes, twisting, leaning like
torsoes of ancient warriors,
tilting, elbowing in at every angle,
as if to point out some moral:
even in death, we all want more room.

How many centuries might a man
or a woman fit in a car?
Last earth holds scalped away,
peeled detritus of dead forests,
night beds of warring clans,
whole families, the oozed bone
masses, drifting ages underground,
to end, at last, fuel for the lonely farmer,
awkward grassy black hulks
sliced with an iron tongue

for a last ride off the planet,
a trip into eternity one night
when a man and a woman grow cold.
Earth warming earth, ashes
ascending from chimneys,
become a question mark of smoke
hanging out above the shore,
as the first lights of the cottages
flicker on and under slate roofs
men and women push their last
pennies into an electric box,
let the damp animals in before
curling under woollen blankets,
toes stretching to make love
to the small knots of clouds
that move up the estuary
in the moonlight, thin white puffs
that drift up like a long white dragon
who hugs the shore, like an image
from a forgotten childhood,
memory of a great parade of kites
or puppets risen from a secret well,
their heaven-clanging music arriving at last
to lift and salt your greying hair.

TEDDY LAVELLE'S

for Tom Cafferkey

Sunday afternoon after the storm

Two boys at the crossroads stand at a fire.
Something black is burning.

They look in through the window;
behind them, the sky eaten by smoke,

brown half-tones of mud and cloud.
Two boys standing by a fire.

Now four girls in white taffeta dresses
walk through the door,
come from their First Communion.

In the back room, the young boys, their brothers,
wave their long wooden cues.
They study the small coloured balls on the table
as if they were boats
              laying out on the green ocean.

Above them, revenuers posed on the wall,
the old woman in black caught at her still.

Two men sing country music at the end of the bar.
In the snug in the corner, three young girls
nurse their Sunday beers. Their eyes
dial long distance numbers to men in foreign countries

In the men's room, a singer nods to a boy,
they stand over the long porcelain urinal, pissing.
Together they look out the window.

More men in suits and straight-backed
women enter the bar.

The soup in its stainless kettle too hot to drink.
Its clear rich broth rising up beneath the cloth
of my children's hands.

Outside the window, at the corner, two boys stand by a fire.
Now they come walking in.

FOR THE OLD WOMAN BY THE ROAD
NEAR THE KIM SON PAGODA

Nobody ever said thank you for picking the soldier up
that night, and carrying his body across the road.

Nobody ever said thank you for lifting the face of the dead
black soldier, closing his eyes and turning his face away.

No one was there to take your picture for the important
books of the war.

Only the green fields stretching out and the blue mountains,
a field of white mist rising off the trees at dawn
that morning when the chopper floated down
to take the bodies.

Sometimes, one of us reaches down and lifts a stranger up
and no one says thank you.

Now your house is the last one left on the road nobody takes.
The scent of burnt temple waters wakes you in the morning.

COMPASS

We carried it in a black metal box like an amulet, or pyx,
walked in strict procession after it,
our heads bent like penitents.

We halted at street corners to watch the magic needle
float up and down, noted carefully
the degrees of variation from true north.

A five-mile hike was out and back to the suburbs.
We took no casualties, except
once at Murphy's Dance Studios,
one boy shot another with an arrow,
his eyes distracted by the long legs of the dancers.

Some of us went to the war.
Some didn't.

One I know died with the black metal box
still stuck in his pocket.

A map of our old neighborhood
swaddled around it.

Because They Will Have to Leave

The sand sculptures the young women have left on the beach
tell of how they will feel on leaving. This one's hollowed
empty eyes could be one of those faces on Easter Island.
It tastes of bitter apple. It says tell me the names
of the birds: pintail, golden eye, grebe, wigeon,
the twenty-five swans on Lough Keel, oystercatcher,
blackbird, cuckoo, plovers like old monks
walking the shore. It is a map
of freezing water.

Because the land can't hold them, with their hands
they spell out messages in the sand. This one
bends to say: tell me the names of the flowers:
fuchsia, rhododendron, meadowsweat, honesty, bog
myrtle, sally rod, lady's mantle, clematis, tormentil,
sun tear. It is a cold
river stream.

Because they will have to leave, they leave messages
for the wind. This one says tell me the names of the places:
Carrickmore, Dooagh, Mweelin, Bunnacurry,
Dugort, Cashel, Keel, Keem, Poolagh, Dookinella,
Dooega, Strahand, Deneen, Caher,
Inishbiggle, Achill Beg, Mweelinda, Craughan, Sliabh Mor,
Knockmore, Inish Galloon. It is a hammer
ringing a life away.

Because they will have to leave, they line the sculptures
along the beaches.
Because they will have to leave, they do not look back.

[In 1995, as part of project with local artists, young women on Achill
Island were asked to create sand sculptures to commemorate the history
of the immigration of women from the island and their own possible
leaving.]

NIGHT WALK: HOAN KIEM

The night arrives in dreams of silken dresses,
sleeveless arms, thin bare legs,

sandals raising a body
forever weightless in the air.

Snaking lights of oncoming cars
stagger dragon-eyed in the dusk.

The city's soft geomancy of love.

Everything always on the point
of entering another landscape.

As if life were only a matter
of bodies and spaces,
there for the light to sing.

In Yeats' Country
for Michael Quirk

All morning, the cows asleep in the fields,
their dazed heads looking up from Castlebar to Sligo,
we get there almost by accident, pass through the green door
of the old butcher shop on Wine St.,
its white porcelain walls, hooks still hanging
from the tin ceiling as if waiting the bodies
of dead animals to descend like manna from heaven.
Michael Quirk, woodcutter, his hands hypnotize
as they move back and forth, fingers skating,
slicing a century's grain and girth. He slides
hammer and chisel gently, never stops talking.
Slivers of skin float to ground. 'Your favorite
animal, quick.' He carves a cheetah for my son,
a cat for my daughter. 'That theosophical crowd,
what could they know,' he asks, 'coming from
where they did.' My daughter treks her song up
and down the Himalayas of the severed trunks
that litter the entrance. The scent of wood
fills the shop. I watch his hands turn as he carves for me
the face of Grace O'Malley. Granuaile.
Right here, not a hundred yards from this place,
he says, she slaughtered a hundred in half an hour.
Hard work. The name, it means island of the Spaniards.
Pirates, they could have no mercy. Soon his hands
cut the circles of eyes that run to pointed breasts,
the armour that covers the walls and doors of pubs for miles.
Below, he carves the *bra son feas*, salmon of knowledge,
and under it the *dogon cu*, the death hound.

I ask if being a butcher has been good training;
he says no, it was his father's business
and when he started cutting wood, the meat just
went flying out the windows. Dizzy walking out
past the old hotel, the swans still gathered at the car
park along the canal, we drive out from the old city,
past the travellers' park on the hill, shirts hung out
like bright crosses on the trees. Half way through
Roscommon, we wake to find we've turned the wrong
direction. Past Newport, the ambulance running at us
down the narrow mountain road, red lights whirling
down the path of the fresh risen moon. Along the sound,
the white faces of the boys in their Warro jackets.
The Rhododendron forest. The House of Prayer.
Brian up on the bog cutting turf in the midnight light.
For days the scent of sycamore on our hands.

WILLIE'S HOUSE
Tisman, Carraroe South

One more endless evening in the West.
The house filled with talk and drink,
scents of burnt fish and potato.

Outside the green door, the white moon pulling
its great weight across the sky.

The cows stretching like wise men in the rock-strewn fields.
The horses asleep in their small circle down by the shore.

The world turning a new colour of blue, filling the rooms,
pushing its way into corners of late night eyes.

Even the words we speak seem to sit softly on blue clouds.

I try to think of a word for it.
Then Lily and Neasa come flying in from the bedroom,
dressed in their mothers' underclothes, their small faces
painted the same deep shade of blue as the air.

All around us the night opening.

Everywhere, this ripening.

HELMETS

We found them hidden down cellars and back
rooms, stuffed in old duffles and lost corners
of closets. They popped out at us, dark clowns
from the war's Jack-in-the-box trunks. We put
our heads in for size, felt their weight and mystery,
drew lots to see who'd be Japs or Nazis.
Some days we listened for sounds of blood red
beaches, boom of guns, the stench of places
whose names were cut in them with jagged teeth-like
letters. A few still wore dents from falling,
or showed holes where hot bullets had passed through,
frayed green remnants of camouflage peeling
off. We wore them in fear of being caught,
a father's shadow looming suddenly
in a door. His look to stop us. Some nights
we woke delirious from chills and fevers,
haunted by scents of saki, snaps, moonshine,
dream-like images of women and children
weeping, the secret labrynthine passages
to death those carved out spaces contained.

BLUES FOR A BASE CAMP SINGER

He can still belt them out like the old days,
'Hey Jude,' 'Proud Mary,'
like those nights in the forsaken bases.
He still remembers the names.
Dau tieng, Tay Ninh, LZ Betty and Jane.
He had the Philipino girls singing back up
behind him then.
Now it's the nightclubs in the cities.
Not duck planks but teak and cherrywood,
an audience that has no idea where he's been.
Still he blasts the songs out.
He's a back-peddling human time machine
in his James Brown suit and dapped hair.
If he'd had his choice he'd have gone back
with the black GIs.,
but tonight he moves through his repertoire,
croons along beside the white piano
thinking of the good days
when there was real pain to touch
the slapping down of mortars,
& hopes of love still moved the world.

Eight True Maps of the West

*i.m. Barbara McDonagh Gilboy, Maire, Brid, and
Martin McDonagh*

1.

*Carraroe, Spiddal, Galway
8 February, 1880*

To the Mansion House Fund
Gentlemen:
 I am entrusted with the spiritual charge of almost 400 fam-
ilies in the district and the island of Lettermullen. It is needless to
unfold the dreadful condition of these poor people who are for
the most part destitute. I say without exaggeration there are 200
families in actual want living on the small consignment of Indian
meal which comes from the Duchess of Marleborough Fund.
There is no one to plead for them except myself and perhaps that
is the worst feature of their condition. We have no cess payer, no
doctor, no rector, in fact no one endowed with the qualifications
required by your committee except myself as clergyman and Mr
McDonagh as Poor Law Guardian. I trust gentlemen that the loss
of such individuals will not entail the further loss of your just con-
siderations.
 Yours faithfully,
 Peter S. Newell

Late afternoon, a half-empty restaurant in the West.
 That time of day   when hope stretches most,
I unwrap the folds of a map,
 across a table something tries to speak,
a hand reaches out from black and white pages,
 extended overlays,   small hesitant dots,
circles of lines to mark the passages of fields and rock,

the wavering fractals of a coast.

Tim Robinson's maps.

If I counted all the microscopic ink spots,
smudges, what might they be:
    a calculus of all the ones who left,
of the ones fallen behind on the roadsides,
    a tabulation of gains and losses,
a calculus of that other universe that exists
    always beside us,
the unnamed ones, the silhouetted faces
tucked with old notes in faded envelopes,
stuck in back of bureau drawers
    in Pittsburgh, Cleveland, Boston,
the names,   the once clear relationships,
    gone forever.

    The sound of them
        opening
            somewhere in space,
            a sea roar.

2.
    Carraroe, Spiddal
      Feb 29th
    Gentlemen
      As we have only one post per week I found it quite
impossible to return the receipt filled according to instructions by
return of post. I beg to remind you that my people are the poor-
est in Irleand and that £25 is a very small amount for their relief

— particularly as so far you have not allowed us a single other
grant. Faithfully Yours,
          Rev. Peter J. Newell

Here, on the page
     the name of that place again.
An Cheathru Rua.   Her place.
A twenty mile ride west from the city,
then the drop   straight down
                   into the peninsula's mouth,
into fields of sandstone, mud,
     Ordivician grit,
         upcroppings of base granite,
     gneiss, Dairadian schists and marbles,
       ending,
             an ocean floor of basalts and cherts.

Casla Bay riding one side, Great Man's Bay, the other.
The bay named for a once plundering giant:

     'his angled rod made of sturdy oak,
     his line a cable which in storms ne'er broke;
     his hook he baited with a dragon's tail,
     and sat upon a rock, and bobbed for a whale.'

An Cheathru Rua Thuaidh.
          Carraroe North.

Somewhere near a fold, an old house.
A picture falling from an envelope.
     An image of a woman and a man
     holding a new-born child.

In the background   a bicycle leaning against
        the white of a cottage.

The sister   who stayed, ageing even then,
        living still amid the hardscrabble
        of old names.

Lochan na Meacan.   Loch na Cora Doite
        Loch Ghleann an Fhir Mhairbh
Lake of the Small Trout.   Lake of the Small Lumps.
        Lake of the Dead Man's Glen.

Cloch na Toirni. The Rock of the Thunder.
Loch an Mhuilinn. The Lake of the Mill.

In a museum in a distant city,
        an artist's painting of the place
        shows a woman in her peasant's dress
                bent over the water,
                        the day's wash
                        laid out along the bank before her.
The painting a wash of lush greens, browns and reds.

What would she have thought who never set foot
into a museum
        but knew the true meaning of that shore,
        knew what would be there in the woman's view
        if she just lifted her eyes?

Oilean an Phriosuin.   The Island of the Prison.
The small island where they took the rent defaulters.
        Place of her night sweats, fears of the poor house.

And there, just over the woman's shoulder,
      Cullion's ridge, here just visible
      as a small line on the map.
Site of the remains of another house:
Kate and John Montague's tumbled down cottage
                              buried in grasses.
Once home to the two sole witnesses at her baptism.
      Place where the fishermen coming down from Cullion
      were frightened into legend one night
      by the ghost
             of the Griffin's tethered donkey.

3.

      Carraroe
      March 21st
Gentlemen
      The Carraroe district contains no townland
which is not in a wretched condition for want of clothes. There are
close on a hundred families for which the children rarely see the out-
erworld but squat round the hearth all day long for want of clothing. I
trust you will make a grant in their favour.
      Peter J. Newell

From this spot only a short walk to the old house & lake.
      Loch na Tamhnaí Móire,
      "Lake of the last arable patch"
but what she would have called, "the Lake of the Big Wind."

Her lake.

its black,   eel-thick waters.
Two swans   moving always
                    across its dark surface.
The small cove behind the house where she went
to wash in the cold waters
            one last time, that night of her leaving.
The news rushed out to the bog where she was working:
            the passage money arrived.
No time even for a gathering. No American wake.

Tonight, somewhere out on the lake, I imagine
            the reflection of her face riding out in the darkness
                    circling frozen under moonless skies,
                            with all those others.

Here on the map I touch the spot.
   The dried ink of the printer,
            marking that place,
                    think of her,
            the dark lake of her lap,
                    she whose trellises
            we climbed at night,
                    fighting to find a place in the folds
                        of her black dresses,
listening to the songs,   the recitations
            of the names of the fields.

Garrái an Locha
      The field of the lake.
Garrái an strúthán.
      The field of the Strand.
Garrái an dórt.

78

The field of the Yellow Seed.
Garrái an Searse.
George's Field.
An Garrái Bán
The White Field.
An Garrái Beag.
The Small Field.
Garrái an sleibhe.
The Hilly Field.
Garrái teach an Talann
The Field of the Salt House.
Garrái an gleanna.
The Glen Field.
Garrái an cladaigh.
The field of the Rocky Shoreline.
Garrái an tseantigh.
The Field of the Old House.

She, not knowing the thousand other fields
        bearing the same names,
knowing only these,
        in all their particularity.

        The common name
            for the common thing.

And the house set amid the clump of trees.
        The miracle of a shelter.
            At the edge of a lake,
        away from the ocean,
            a house of thatch and stone,
two families, twenty odd bodies

living together among the animals.

A life locked between waters.
　　　A lake on one side.
　　　　　An ocean on the other.

A people of water and rock.　　A hard people.
Deep.
　　　Tidal.
　　　　　Impenetrable?

4.

　　　　　Carraroe
　　　　　　May 10th
Dear Gentlemen:
I enclose receipt for goods purchased for £10 which was granted
by your Committee towards purchasing clothes for the poor of
my district. The receipt is not for the whole amount as I had to
reserve money to pay an old woman who made some of the arti-
cles however if required I can get a receipt for that too.

　　　As that is the only grant I received for that purpose from
any source and as I did not participate in the general distribution
of such articles conducted by His Royal Highness I trust you will
consider my claims to your charity for a community in greatest
distress to be difficult to find — Anxiously awaiting a grant for
either food or clothes
　　　　　　I am Gentlemen
　　　　　　　Yours Faithfully
　　　　　　　　Peter J. Newell
　　　　　　　　　Areas Carraroe Re: Com.

A finger space down: the small square marker.
    Caladh Tadhg.
The old stone pier.   The place where a boy once pulled
    from the edge of the sea
    the 6,000 year old antler
of a Great Irish deer,   took it to the local schoolmaster
    who sent it to the museum   in Dublin
where it sits still   tagged and lonely in a drawer.

Place where she spent her nights cleaning fish,
    hands sleeked with entrails, secrets
    of the gleaming bodies
        the dark boats riding on the tides,
        hookers that once sailed turf to the Arans.
    Boats sold when the hard times came.
        Patrick Griffin's, *The Swan.*
    Boats scattered now,
    a few surviving, refurbished, red sails and black hulls
        rolling restless in the bays.

Boats. Her own father's boat. *The Patacan.* The Hare.
    Its hull of blackened pine   sailing on
    until Debbie
        wrapped its arms around her.
                                    1961.
                A few months after her own crossing.

Here, if I pressed my ear to the page,
I wonder would I hear the sound of the old night talk,
    the voices singing, stories retold?

Would I hear the sound of the constable's steps

81

as he moved down the road that night:
         April 1.   Year 1   of the new century,
hear his fingers tapping anxiously
         at the blue grids of the census book,
   waiting to take inventory of the cottage.

Material: stone.   Roof: thatch.   Windows: one.
Occupants: Sean McDonagh.   Age: 52.
Occupation: Farmer.   Religion.   Roman Catholic.
   Language: Irish.
Cecilia McDonagh: Farmer's Wife
Age 48.   Religion: Roman Catholic. Language: Irish.

   Moving down the line to Ann, 19. Daughter.
Language: Irish & English. (Already the languages mixing.)
         Coleman, 21.   Farmer.   Language: Irish & English.
         Last, the old woman.   Mary. Age, 92,
(whose name she gave her daughter.)

But there on the page, no mention of the children gone.
   Not Máire   Bríd   Mártín   Barbara.
Did they all wake that night
         to hear the sound of the pen crossing the page,
declaring forever their exile
         as Mr. Thomas Sullivan, constable,
               held out the document,
waiting for Sean, to affirm it
         with his mark, his x,
before moving on to the other half of the house,
               the family of Matthias Griffin?

5.

Carraroe

Gentlemen:

Please consider the number and amount of grants made to our committee this season — you will find them rather small considering the district and the number of families. I have received no grants since I returned accounts so there is no use in repeating ciphers. The families are exhausted. The people are miserable and there seems no immediate prospect of amelioration. I would not consider my duty to my people discharged if I were not to inform you of their condition. I have done so twice lately to no purpose. I must say briefly they are in the want and the rest remains with you.

Yours faithfully,

Peter Newell

Further out   just visible at the turn of the bay
   the small island.   *Inis Mhic Conaith.*
The place they went to escape the hunger
   and the taxes.
Place of terrible storms.
   The old woman moving through the house
   sprinkling holy water,
   act repeated how many times
      in cramped apartments in a new country.

On the island still the sites of the lazy beds,
   the hillocks, Proinnsias O'Flartha's castle,
     the sole two storey structure.
        Occupied until the last inhabitant
        sailed off the islands in the 70's

Here, Mairtin Kirwin,
        the rate collector,   demanding
            his tenants sail out to meet him with their rents,
the site of his coming and going on the mainland
            kept always   a secret.
His boat steered carefully to avoid   the currents
                        and rocks.

Carrag an Liagain. Carrag an Ime.   Lagan Ime.
        Cora na Móna.

And here, the first landfall on the mainland.
    Michael Flaherty's house,
        his seven daughters
    sweeping in and out of the rooms
that day he first sailed me out to the island,
    where I walked through the empty rooms
        of the old house,
    touched the black imprint where the fires
        scorched the walls.
The way back in, the small engine of his boat
    churning up the waters
        the currach crowded with sheep,
    passing the markers,
            the last shoals and rocks,
    place of the famine graves.

And here and there, the other markers set
                across the peninsula.
Teach an Tae,   the House of Tea,
from where they tried to feed the hungry, sick, and dying.
    The sites of holy wells and streams.

Strathan an Bheannaithe.   Stream of the Blessing.
      Ceibh a Tstruthan an Bheannaithe.
            Island of the stream of the blessing.

Place where a line of saints once stopped off
      from their journeying,
      placed their loads down   on the land
            left a string of looping markers,
                  a stone rosary.

Other marks, barely visible: sites of burial mounds,
      hillocks of shells, remnants of fires,
            shadows of huddled eaters.

Places of the burning of seaweed, the kelp
      making for an industry, a living for a time,
   its export   for the manufacture of iodine bringing
      some prosperity   through the Great War,
until the discovery   of other ways to treat the
wounded.

Later, the textile mills, the tax incentives   for industry,
      the plant manufacturing perfume decanters
the detritus still scattered,
      old bottles lifted from the grasses by children
      to play with as guns.

Finally, the arrival of hard wiring.
      The radio station.

An Cheathru Rhua.   The Red land.
     Land of red sky.   Red faces.
          Red hardened bodies.

6.

          Carraroe
               May 10th
Dear Sir:
  I am writing by the post to the Mansion House Committee sol-
liciting a grant for my poor people and as I have had experience of
your kindness on a former occasion I venture once more to be-
seach your favour and support. At the Instigation of Lord Francis
Osborne I wrote to you before and it was the only time I received
a very liberal grant.
     I am similarly unfortunate as regards those gunboats and
have not yet received any clothes from that source though the
other clergymen in the neighboring parishes have received some
15 or 20 bales of such articles. The gentleman in whose hands the
distribution is placed — I mean Major Gaskell — from some rea-
son or other has not thought it convenient either to let my people
have them or to visit them and see if they were required as he has
done to the other districts. This I mention not by way of censure
but merely to explain why I am applying now to your committee.
I hope you will pardon the trouble I cause you and have the hon-
our to
                    Remain
               Yours Truly
                    Peter J. Newell

At last, the map's lines thinning,
     the road climbing to the barracks.

"The first slated house, built 1840"

We thought it a fiction,
        the creation of an addled,
                dying brain.
The shadow on the road
        always in the stories.

Two hundred yards beyond: the Macklin's House.
        The site of the battle.

Cath na Ceathrún Ruaidth.
        The Battle of Cararroe.   1880.

The bad years. Rents jumping. 5 pounds. 10 pounds.
A compensatory rise in the manufacture of poitin.
A peninsula of 2,000 acres.   100 acres tillable.
The census count:
        4 horses, 15 donkeys, 120 cows, 52 sheep,14 pigs.

A steady rise in evictions.
        Soon, along the roadsides
                the growing preparations.
                        The pails of boiling water readied. The fires.
At the Macklin's house, the first collectors sent off.
        The next day the soldiers returning,
                                Mrs. Macklin
        waving her shovel of hot coals.

Four hundred women, and children, Davitt claimed.
        gathered and waiting.
Sixty soldiers charging,   bayoneting,

striding forward   into the fall of rocks   and coals
           buckets of boiling water
                               following them.

Body count: 1 killed. Scores more wounded.
     Many, women and children.

Six months later the 'City of the Tribes,'
     sailing into Casla Bay,
   weighted down with 200 police and soldiers.

"The Carraroe Affair" Lord Oranmore Brown called it.

Six years old, was she there?
        Hanging at her mother's side
             forever astounded
                 by the movement of the crowd?
A memory of it ingrained, a rock hard striation
     made in the brain.
A fold entered forever.
        A fear of police and soldiers.

7.

Carraroe
June 4th

Dear Sir:

    I have received my letter returned because you say — it
had not the No. inscribed. Now the communication must have
been easily traceable as the No is always placed by us on the enve-
lope. I hope the application for relief already made holds good
and that the present note is formal.

East, toward Rossiveel, the ferry point.
Black escarpments cut into hillsides.
Coves,   smugglers' havens,   white sand beaches.

Here, the old church and graveyard.
        The place they sailed for Mass.
        The *cillin*. The stone church
                built overnight by a journeying saint.
Teampaill Ins' MacaAidaimh
        Called 'Church of the Sons of Adam,'
                in O'Donovan's Survey.
Saint Mocan's.   Saint from the Arans.
        And Proinnsias O'Flatharta's grave inside?

At the entry, the stone water font
        filled with rain water
        birds flying in and out of ivy, weaving
                        threadlike   through   rock.

Tra na Reilige .
The graveyard by the beach,
        its wild scatterings of markers:
                white sand, glassed-in   flowers,
        pink statues,   stone offerings.

Charles Lamb, the painter, his stone bench
        set up at the crest,
                even in death claiming the artist's prospect,
                looking out forever

89

                    across the landscape,
the stone graves and bathers,
        the tourists ferrying back and forth   to the islands.
Dead center of the graveyard:
        the single stone marker for the islanders.
        The unmarked graves
        of Sean, Cicily, Ann, Mary, Coleman.
        Did they feel us there that sun drenched afternoon:
           the three of us, three men drawn from the blood
        of those same brothers and sisters,
                        men separated by an ocean' century,
           staring out in silence
             at the mystery
                of that green   leave-taking sea?

8.

        Mansion House Committee
              for the Relief of Distress in Ireland
                 Revd P. J. Newell: Sec
                 Lettermullen & Carraroe
                     Oughterard
                         Co. Galway
Dear Rvd Sir:
        In reply to your communication which arrived here this
morning I beg to inform you that it is not sufficient to mark the
number only on the envelope, as the communications are so nu-
merous, and pass through such a number of hands that they are
very likely to get mislaid unless this inscription appears on every
document. It is the only way we possess in tracing your commit-
tee, and you will therefore take especial care in future to stamp
all communication with 594 595.
        I am

                            90

Faithfully Yours
J. C. Lyons
Registrar

Southward finally, the last turnings of the bay,
        the peninsula bending toward its final reach of rock,
beds of pink-white, bud-like sand.

An Doolin.   The Coral Strand.
The white of the beach. What could be bone.
The pink white of the Lithothamnium.
        Tiny forks   of fossilized seaweed,
        like small   milk white   hands   reaching up.

Cormac's Stone. The children's graveyard
        dug up when the road was widened.
Famine graves.

'It never happened there,' she told us.
        But now I have touched the graves,
                seen the pictures.
The photo in the National Library.
"A starving Irish family from Carraroe, during the famine."

The house in the picture, the dirt floor, the wooden cradle,
        it could be hers.
And the seven figures lying there, who were they?
The father who sits holding a child in his arms,
        a blanket wrapped tight   around them.
The other children with bird-like faces,
        narrowing jaws, foreheads stretching.
The mother slumped on the floor,

head resting on one of the two remaining
     pieces of furniture.
Behind them   the damp, cracked walls,   glowing
          like a map of the hungry world.
They sit as if caught in the midst of some halo,
     the looks on their faces, captured forever staring
          into the circle of light
          made by what must have been
          the photographer's flash
               going off inside the cottage.

Southward still now. The last channel out.
Here, the memories of a night gathered by a fire,
          each one of us,   armed with a pen
trying to draw a map,
                    the best way out of the city.
By the grate, our pencils moving,   hands drawing in
          the nubs and crosses, lines circling, climbing,
               making fishfalls,
                         inlets,
recreating a world of indents, thumb scratches,
          folds within folds, ghost etchings,
               smudges of history lost,
fighting to trace the best route south
          to the airport to pick up a grandaughter
               who carried her name.

Who could forget the wild geography of it:
          The one page running
               to the next.
The eight roundabouts out of Galway City,
          like the eight glorious mysteries,

the eight feats of prowess
required to break free of the undertow
    of a land pulled so wildly from the grasp
        of the deep blue sea,

a land traced here again,   light fading,
street players, retuning their instruments,
            a map refolded, tucked into a folder
            in a still half empty restaurant,
                at the edge of the lonesome west.

Note:
    The lyrics for the "Giant of Greatman's Bay" are from Roderic
O'Flaherty's *A Chronological Description of H-Iar Connacht (1684)*.
Other sources are from Tim Robinson's *Connemara, a Map and Gaze-
teer*. The *Census Report of 1901*; Michael Davitt's *The Death of Feudal-
ism in Ireland*, and Raymond Standun and Bill Long's *Singing Stone /
Whispering Wind: Voices of Connemara*. For the letters of Peter Newell
to the Mansion Committee I am indebted to my cousin, Máire McDon-
agh of Carraroe, to Liam Ó Mainnín and to Tomas Griffin for the
history of Carraroe and Inchemekinna.

CLIMBING TO HUNG TEMPLE

What could they have thought of us,
    those women sitting out in line,
waiting at the steps of the temple,
    bent over in that strange, familiar way;
what could they
    have thought of us
when they saw us
    walking up the path

with those other pilgrims, our bodies leaning,
    wading through the heat,
all morning praying our way up the mountain,
    lifting our legs
along the steepening track,
    prying soles loose from the kiss
of red black mud,
    & gnarled, ancient roots,

dragged up the mountain years ago,
    praying our way past
the outstretched bloated
    bodies of blood worms;
each of us lost in thought,
    surprised by the faces
of the young children
    and women who stepped from the forest,

beggars and vendors selling incense,
    medallions, fans, plastic necklaces
of the Buddha.

94

Out of breath, we struggled
to climb the last steps
    to the clearing,
almost at the end of our pilgrimage,
    a cluster of low-crouched temple houses,

those old women waiting,
    sitting in that ageless way,
hems of their trousers kissing the dirt,
    brown shirts and turbans
bleached in dust, handkerchiefs
    used in that old back and forth
motion, fanning themselves,
    brushing away the sweat, the heat of the day.

We took their gifts of joss sticks
    & pushed our way into
smoke-filled halls,
    inner rooms of pilgrims, bodies
twisting in white vapors.
    We stopped to bow at the shrines,
placing our sticks of incense in the pots,
    guessing, not yet knowing, which

were for the princesses,
    which the lesser gods,
squeezed like the poor
    into the corners.
Not a word between us, not even
    outside, where the crowd,
a sheet of color,
    gathered by the small black stele,

lighting the last few joss sticks,
    setting them, lone sentinels,
in the sand, leaning
    back to seek shelter from the burning
white sheet of the sun,
    then sitting with the others,
hunched at the ledges of the court yard,
    their humble lunches spread out,

letting go for a single hour
    the mysteries of our separate selves.
What could they have thought of us
    when they saw us there, those old women,
staring out across the clearing,
    staring through that airless space,
the ghost bodies
    of their missing sons?

FEEDING ANNA FUCHS' GOATS

The creak of a gate opening.

Upon a post, a sign:
'if you cross over this threshold
you have visited an Irish farm.'

Inside, the dark orifice,
tumbled- in hives of sheds
& wind-battered buildings.
A leaf strewn pool running black
through the chicken coup.

Eneas and Wendy already at work in the mud.
Wendy in the barn trying to lure two kids
who've broken in the door in the night,
a fat black cat staring down from a worm-eaten rafter.

Eneas with Anna's thirty goats at the feed trough,
nudging the younger ones in to the bin.
The pen, a nacrous world of vapours, rain water,
goat breath, fresh running streams of urine.

A soft rain falling across the mountainside,
sending up scents of hay, souring milk
toward the Megalithic tombs just visible in the mist.

The riprap of the rain on rock and water a song, a soft
urging at the throat. The world, a dark green labyrinth,
a nest tucked in the arm of the mountainside.
Once entered, there is no way out.

THE LE THAI GARDENS

History rode through here
on a black horse
& cut down everything in sight:
the women at the well,
the dog in the yard;
it had no mercy.

All day men fell like rain from the sky
& women wept
as guns lifted the lids from their eyes.

Who will us give us back our children?
the women asked,

but the men turned their backs
like helmets to the walls
& shut out
their terrible screaming.

At night now the men's hands
become great baskets of fish
laughing up at them
& the coma
they have yet to fall out of.

ALUMINIUM

He stood straight in front of the camera in a gray fitted suit.
He spoke slowly in a clipped Cambridge accent.
He had a name that conjured marbled stairs
winding up to exhibit halls,
gloved hands held extended, coats of arms, cordials, sherry.
Each Sunday he introduced us to the play, the song,
the performance.
We gathered to stare at the black box, watching this thing
which he said was our culture.
At intermissions he stepped into the circle of light
to introduce the sponsor.
We sat back, smiled with satisfaction at the way
he said the word. *Aluminium.*
Miracle metal of the space age, whose lightness
sent our planes and rockets hurtling, kept our foods,
like our lives, safely preserved.
Later in school we learned it was forged from an ore
pulled from mines in distant countries
whose names our host had never thought to mention.

BORNEO

It was the name of that place
from where the man in our
nightmares would come to
get us. The dark bearded
one the nuns and our parents
threatened us with those times
when we didn't obey,
whose existence our grandmothers
confirmed when in the confines
of small apartments
we got too wild.
Oh, he would come to get us
in all his glory, they warned,
bones jutting out from cheeks
and ears, necklaces made
from children's teeth jangling
at his bearded neck, hair
hanging half way down to eternity.
Nights we conjured routes of escape,
fought for the space in the bed by the wall.
Afternoons, we watched the way
our grandmothers looked
at us as they sat by the windows,
the way they suddenly turned
their eyes up the street, as if
half-expecting his arrival
from those distant jungles
years later a few of us
would visit and help burn.

WAR'S SEASON
October, 2002

First cold spell of the fall.
The frost settling in over the yards.
The last plants waiting the sun to arrive
as down the coast men debate
the logic of a war they say
will come upon us as surely
as the next season.
Hollow speeches of empty men bang
off walls of empty chambers.
Good men and women try to speak up
and are silenced.
They hear already the sound of coins
falling one by one into metered slots,
wake to the noise of the distant engines
starting up in the morning.
They fear it is Death is behind the wheel,
once more hungry for his harvest.

DEATH COMES TO THE BARRACKS

for Charles Simic

Death comes to the barracks.
All the soldiers are sleeping.
Death tiptoes past their beds,
studies the faces, the pale and the robust.
Death runs his hands over
the peach fuzz of a new conscript.
He tries to think of a young girl,
a child he can match with him.
Death walks the polished aisles.
Bunk by bunk, he takes note
of who has spit shined boots,
or polished brass. Death waits
until he knows the young men
sense his presence before leaving.
he sighs for them all: the ones
he will take as well as the ones
he will spare. All night Death
travels, barracks to barracks,
field to field, country to country.
Death blesses himself as he passes
the great stone houses of those
whom he will give long life.
Only toward dawn does Death return home,
his body aching and tired, each night
his pockets weighted down with the names
of more and more of his sad recruits.

SHIPWRIGHTS

for Sean the Shore

By the edge of the shore two brothers at work
shaving fresh cut boards to repair the broken hull
of a red Achill yawl. My son and I moved past
two small dogs barking as we skirted the fence.
All morning I had sensed a fierce questioning
burning in my son's chest. When we'd passed
he looked up and told me his quandary: "If a kind
man raised a vicious dog would it still be mean?"
he asked. I looked away to the fields, wondering
was it the dogs, or something I had done or said,
that had brought on this questioning. I told him,
"No. It is not necessarily true. A dog might still
grow up kind." I think he sensed a hesitation in
my voice, and so persisted, asking after a pause:
"If a mean man raised a kind dog would it in turn
become mean?" I confessed I did not have an answer,
but that good dogs could survive such things
and turn out true and kind. He looked at me as if
satisfied for the time being with my makeshift answering.
Off the bog we turned to watch a flock of linnets taking off,
followed them, our eyes pulled by their motion back
down to the shore. We could see them there still,
the two men off in the distance, like figures in
an ancient painting, hard at work, despite the coming storm.